DAYS IN DEVONPORT
Part IV

Gerald W. Barker

Prorsum Semper Honeste

Straight on always to Honourable Achievement, is the motto on Devonport's Arms. The Grant of Arms on 6th November, 1876, was a mark of honour which greatly stimulated the ever-growing civic pride at this period. A fine copy executed in stained glass was to be seen in one of the rooms of Devonport Guildhall. The Naval Crown appears in many Grants of Arms for distinguished maritime services, but Devonport had a further mark of distinction in having a second crown in the crest. Dolphins (sacred to Neptune) are shown at the top and, at the bottom, a ship in the course of building. A part of the crest can be seen on the badge of Devonport High School for Boys' blazers.

This version of the book is virtually as originally published, presenting the work of Gerald W Barker. There are now additional pages at the back providing information about the publisher, Arthur L Clamp.

The republishing project is being managed by Arthur's grandson, Steven Gibson. We aim to find all the research that he was involved in publishing, preserving it for the next generation as part of 'The Clamp Collection'.

INTRODUCTION

"I did not go out after bell ringing. I never was out over the draw-bridge after six o'clock and that is the truth." John Richards, in his defence, said that he could not, therefore, have been near the bridge at the bottom of Stoke Damerel Churchyard soon after nine o'clock on the evening of Saturday, 21st July, 1787. He was, however, found guilty along with William Smith of the murder of Mr. Phillip Smith, a clerk in the Survey Office of the Dockyard. Thousands of people waited around the gibbet that stood on the banks of the creek near Millbridge to see the bodies, previously executed at Heavitree gallows in Exeter, taken from the cart and hung in iron cages where they stayed for seven years.

The draw-bridge in Fore Street (the principal street) stood in the vicinity of where the main entrance to Devonport Park now is. Fore Street was approached from the direction of Stoke Damerel Church through a limestone arched gateway. During the reign of George II, 1727-1760, huge barriers and fortifications were raised around the town. The King's Boundary walls constituted lines of fortifications 12 feet high on the north and south-east. The walls of the Dock Wharf were in some places 30 feet high; and those of the Gun Wharf protected the town on the north-west. The heavy batteries at Mount Wise protected the entrance from the sea, and the redoubt and block house on Mount Pleasant commanded the capital of the lines, within which were extensive Barracks, the Government House and Port Admiral's House. Other fortifications existed. These included a breastwork with a ditch from 12 to 20 feet deep excavated from the solid slate and limestone rock. The ditch extended from the vicinity of Buff Battery, which is a little way up the hill from Stonehouse Bridge across the Brickfields near the spot where the steps are and across to where the main entrance to the park is now. It continued across the park behind the park keeper's lodge and ended at New Passage Hill. Locals remember the "moat", behind Devonport Hospital, that was used as a rifle range, and was in existence long after the war until it became filled-in for use as a car-park.

Where the "dip" in the Dockyard wall occurs in New Passage Hill, leading up to Marlborough Street, is the area in which another fosse drawbridge stood. The third landward approach into the town stood at the Main Guard on Devonport Hill. This approach from Stonehouse, unlike the other two land entrances, had no barrier gates. These were left unfinished after an inspection by the Duke of Wellington in 1816.

Being a sentry on duty at these fortifications was no sinecure. A local sentry was killed whilst on duty. John Richards, who was executed for his part in the Stoke Damerel Churchyard murder, was suspected of killing the sentry. Another sentry on duty at the guard-house on Devonport Hill was overcome by the effect of the blizzard on 8th March, 1891. The sentry box was blown over in the force ten wind. The sentry had to be taken to the nearby barracks to recover and thaw out.

In the early twenties, when Fore Street was widened, workmen uncovered some underground tunnels that had been extremely well constructed. They were in the vicinity of the main entrance to Devonport Park and believed to have been part of the town's fortifications. Mr. Arthur Rickard recalls the great interest aroused by the find and of the numbers of Dockyard workmen who took an interest in the excavation after finishing work.

Mr. Arthur Clamp has always been mentioned last in previous *Days in Devonport* books, but on this occasion will be first, if only for his contribution of the layout of Devonport with its fortifications in the centre pages. My thanks also to Mr. R. Rundell, Secretary of the Hertfordshire Postcard Club, Mr. G. Fleming, Mrs. J. R. Gribbell, Mr. G. Sloggett, Mr. R. Watkins, Mrs. V. Anstis, Miss M. Gordon, Mrs. W. Rogers, Mr. R. W. Ellery, Miss L. M. Hooper, Mr. C. Symons, Mr. P. F. Ghillyer, Mr. J. Williams, Mrs. B. Couch, Mr. H. Feabes, Mr. R. Smith, Mr. R. Baser, Mr. A. Baser, Mr. F. R. Bundy, Mr. T. H. Reed, Mr. D. Hooper and Mrs. C. Gardner. Book V will include a number of early photographs of the Devonport (Royal Albert Hospital) now being demolished.

Gerald W. Barker,
44 Burnhall Park Road,
Peverell, Plymouth
Telephone 784725
July, 1983

Appendix

Boyhood Memories of Devonport was written by Roy Watkins. Pages 14 and 15, Book III. Roy Harris adds the names of: Ron Elliot, Cliff Mules and Cliff Bastin to the 1946 football team. Page 16, Book II. The Carnival Queen's maid was Miss Eileen Barrett. Page 5, Book II.

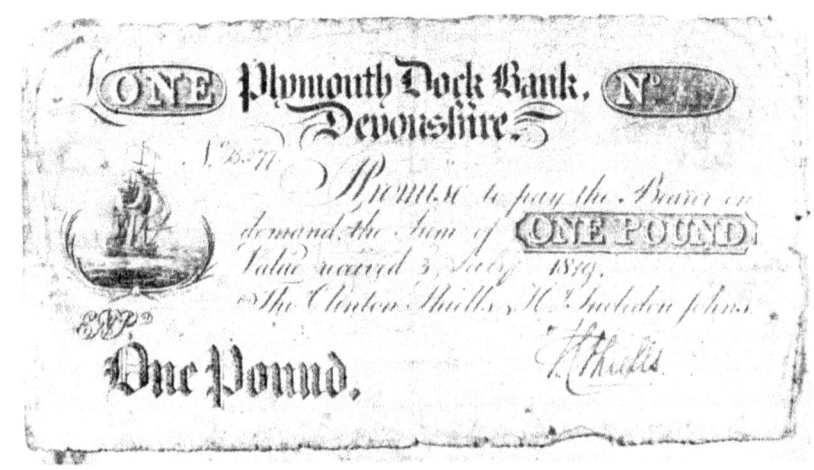

Dinner Time!

Sam Tremain's carriages are a part of this dinner-time scene in Fore Street. They were based in the Stoke Mews, behind the pub on the corner of Stoke village called *Stoke Inn*, and also at the back of Nelson Gardens. Devonport had numerous horses. Many sturdy steeds were also stabled in the vicinity of the car park near Belmont Church. Note the row of lights outside "Aggies" (Royal Sailor's Rest). The building inside the Dockyard's South Gate is the cashier's office. The Church of St. Lo is on the right. Before Gamlens moved to join David Sale on the north side, enabling "Aggies" to extend, Devonport's busiest cab-rank was opposite Gamlens.

The Devonport "Rest"

When a big Co-operative store became vacant in Fore Street in 1874 Miss Agnes Weston rented it for one year with the option of purchase at the end of that time. Before the toilets were built at the top of Catherine Street it was the site of the well-known Island House, which consisted of apartments where people lived. As there was at one time only a toilet in the market and another in Devonport Park, Mr. C. E. Niles (one of those who opposed the amalgamation of the Three Towns in 1914) suggested the need for public conveniences to be built. So in 1924 the shoppers in Devonport found underground toilets, similar to those adjacent to Derry's Clock, had been constructed. Ginger Rendle, a little further down the hill, would swallow watches and ask the sailors to listen to the ticking. In the early twenties spectators would watch him swallowing swords.

Telephone No. 437.   WORKS: GRANBY STREET.

HIORNS and MILLER,

Navy & Army Printers & Publishers,

Stationers, Bookbinders and Rubel Stampers,
Naval and Military Photographers, etc.

Ordnance, Cycling and Motor Maps and Guide Books
Large and select stock of Leather Goods of every description
Stationery in all its Branches.

107, Fore Street, Devonport.

Hiorns and Miller

Long before the first Woolworths appeared Hiorns and Miller, stationers at 107 Fore Street, had 6½d. bazaars, where glass and china basins, and rows of yellow mixing bowls, were ranged around the floor.

Evacuation Group, 1944

Mrs. J. R. Gribbell, née Baldwin, the present Churchwarden of St. Aubyn's Church was standing in the back row on the extreme right of this Stoke Damerel High School group. They had been evacuated to Truro. The girls were members of the Red Cross. Other girls in the photo included: Marian Rundell, Annie Cottell, Eileen Earl, Sylvia Pugh, Marion Couch and Margaret Parker. The school was used for a time by the Royal Naval Artificer Apprentices before moving to their new home in Torpoint, later to be known as H.M.S. *Fisgard*.

Reverend Johnson, 1920s

Two thousand pounds were required in the late 1920s for the restoration of the East window of St. Aubyn's Church. St. Aubyn Chapel, as it was originally known, was erected in Chapel Street in 1771. It consisted of nave, aisles, western tower and low spire. The then Rector of Stoke Damerel strongly opposed the grant of a Chapel of Ease, and, as a compromise, was empowered to prevent marriages or baptisms from taking place.

Choir in Procession

The choir of St. Aubyn's Church is seen in procession on Ascension Day, 1926. It was the day when the unveiling of the East window took place. There is a brass plaque to commemorate the event inside the church. A part of the Rose window was removed to Torquay during the 1939–45 war for safe keeping. The minister's name was Reverend Arthur Johnston. Others remembered were: Harold Grunsell, Maurice Hurdon and Leonard Baldwin. The church hall was a little way up Chapel Street past the taxis sign next to Perkins the undertakers.

Who's for Tennis?

A group from St. Aubyn's Church who are probably more content with a relaxing char-a-banc ride.

St. Aubyn's Choir

This group assembled in the early 1950s for the photographer among whom are Roberts, Galliford, Ted Grunsell, Mr. Leader, Rev. John D. Llewelyn, Len Baldwin, Mr. Hughes, organist, C. Cocks, verger, Y. Samuels, Rose Hatterly, Jean Winsor, June Winsor, Cox, Cox, Grunsell, G. Harvey, G. Wright and L. Hughes.

Blockhouse

Also known as *Mount Pleasant Redoubt*, Blockhouse is situated near Stoke village. At the highest point in the borough when it was constructed in the reign of George II, it commanded the capital of the lines within which were extensive Barracks. Magnificent views of the Breakwater, Sound, River Tamar, Naval Base and ships in harbour, Dartmoor hills, Mount Edgcumbe, Cornish hills, Saltash and bridge plus Gunnislake and Torpoint can be obtained. It affords one of the most extensive and picturesque views in the city. One of the first of the anti-aircraft guns in the Second World War was sited at Blockhouse. At the bottom of the slope in the photo, towards Pasley Street, ran the Devonport Leat, which began on Dartmoor. Not far away a viaduct carried some of the leat water, in the vicinity of Alcester Street, over the railway lines to a reservoir near Herbert Street.

Ford, Devonport

Ram the Ram
(with variations)

Mrs. Christine Gardner remembers as a girl, men with black faces on Boxing Day singing in Browning Road, Stoke, near Pasley Street, the following song. As they sang they carried orange decorated trees and collected for charity. They wore clothes made out of old curtains and tissue paper:

> Ram the Ram, King of the Bush,
> He sold his wife for a pair of shoes,
> And when the shoes began to wear,
> The dirty old man began to swear.
> He rolls them up
> And he rolls them down
> And he rolls them all around the town.
> But when the shoes began to wear,
> The dirty old man began to swear.

The song was sung to the tune of *The Irish Washer Woman*.

TEN SHILLINGS REWARD.

WHEREAS some evil-disposed Boys or other Persons, have been breaking Glass and damaging Scaffolding, &c., belonging to the Building, 17, Pasley Street, Morice Town. This is to give Notice that any Person giving Information to Mr. J. JEFFERIES, Builder, 13, Herbert-street, Morice Town, as shall lead to the conviction of the Offender or Offenders, shall receive the above Reward.

SAMUEL AND JOHN KEYS, PRINTERS, 46, ST. AUBYN STREET, DEVONPORT.

KIMBER'S GARAGE
Albert Road Devonport

Repair Specialists

Motor Engineers

Authorised Dealers for

Austin, Ford and Hillman Cars

Cellulose Painting

Large Stock of Tyres and Accessories.

Catherine Street

The lower part of the street before widening out at the top of the hill where the Royal Sailors' Rest was situated. J. B. Love's building can be seen with the clock on the top. On the right, P. A. Norman, known locally as *Pan Norman*, had a wall advertisement. He had a music shop in 16 Albert Road. He was a "toff" and would be seen with spats, velvet coat and bowler hat plus a smart velvet collar. His shop, opposite the Methodist Chapel, was full of sheet music. The gateway, one of a number into Devonport Market, is on the right hand side of the photo. The name *Fredman* was well known in Devonport. Myer Fredman was Devonport's penultimate Mayor, 1911-1912.

Showing the Flag

Proudly showing the flag displaying the name *J. B. Love*. This well remembered shop was at the bottom of busy Catherine Street. *Jimmy Love's Emporium* spread around the corner towards old Edinburgh Street. The building was huge and was thronged with customers. It matched Jimmy Tozer's and Bould's shops. Jimmy Love was a very popular shop manager with the people of Devonport. The tall beautiful roofs were all done in wrought iron in Victorian style. This once beautiful building was destroyed in the blitz. Jimmy Love served as a magistrate on the Council.

Wash Day, 1920s Style

Wash day in the courtyard of 45 Duke Street. Mr. Voss and Mrs. Polly Voss are with their daughter, Mrs. Florence Davey, and Ann Baldwin. Wash day was usually on a Monday and many a boy and girl would hungrily wait for tea while the huge rollers of the mangle would squeeze the water out of the clothes when the handle was turned.

Harry Claff Presents...

Harry's picture is in the front of the Hippodrome. The operatic novelty being presented by Harry Claff is entitled, *The White Knight*. The poster is advertising next Sunday's Military Concert by the Band of the Royal Marines. Mr. Cyril Symons, who still completes skilful signwriting posters, painted the letters "HIPPO" on the slates of the roof. The roof was not wide enough to allow the full name "HIPPODROME" to be completed owing to the projection room that was situated in the roof. "HIPPO" could clearly be seen by those people walking up Chapel Street.

Room for One Single and Two Doubles

The grandfather of Mrs. V. Anstis and Miss M. Gordon of Devonport was Albert Reed. He was the commissionaire of the Hippodrome before it became a cinema in 1932, having been built as a variety theatre in 1902. He was also a commissionaire of the Electric before the talkies. The name *Hippodrome* is worn on the front of the cap that Albert Reed is wearing.

DEVONPORT CORPORATION. 1914

COMMITTEES.

Cemetery—Alderman Jolliffe. Councillors Essenhigh, Heard, Hellen, Jackson, Jenkin, W. J. May, W. S. May, Mayne, Olver, Perkins, Rudall, Screech, Smith, R. Tozer Ware, and Watson.

Distress—Aldermen Cousins, Goldsmith, Hornbrook, and Waycott. Councillors Archer, Baxter, Clarke, Daymond, Heard, Jenkin, Mayne, and Moses. Guardians—Mr. T. A. Dolton, Rev. A. T. Head, Messrs. J. Ledley, W. J. May, W. H. Roberts, C. Wall, Mrs. K. Davey, Mrs. P. Smith. Co-opted Members—Messrs. J. K. Brenton, W. H. Mounstephen, Mrs. K. M. Steele, Mr. J. A. Symons, and Rev. C. R. Teape.

Electric Power—Aldermen Day and Love. Councillors Baxter, Clarke, Essenhigh, George, Goodman, Jane, Jenkin, W. S. May, McDonald, Treglohan, Viggers, Weakford, Ware, and Welsford.

Finance—Aldermen Gill, Hornbrook, and Love. Councillors Chappell, Clarke, Cramer, Fredman, George, Hocking, Mayne, McDonald, Moon, Perkins, Rudall, Weakford, and Welsford.

Free Public Library—Aldermen Goldsmith, Jolliffe, and Waycott. Councillors Baxter, Chappell, Cramer, Essenhigh, George, Jackson, Jenkin, W. S. May, Olver, Perkins, Roberts, Treglohan, and Ware. Members not in Council, Rev. A. J. Conibear, Rev. H. R. Kruger, Messrs. J. Ledley and G. G. Wood.

Gas—Aldermen Cousins, Hornbrook, Jarvis, Leest, and Tozer. Councillors Charlick, Cole, Daymond, Doney, Fredman, Heard, Jenkin, Mayne, Moses, Phillips, and Watson.

Housing—Alderman Goldsmith. Councillors Baxter, Chappell, Doney, Essenhigh, Jackson, Jane, Jenkin, W. J. May, Mayne, Olver, Perkins, Screech, R. Tozer, Weeks, and Welsford.

Landing Stages—Alderman Day. Councillors Chappell, Clarke, Essenhigh, Goodman, Heard, Hellen, Jackson, Jane, Mayne, Olver, Screech, R. Tozer, Ware, Watson, and Weeks.

Lands—Aldermen Cousins, Fredman, Leest, Littleton, and Risdon. Councillors Doney and Weeks.

Lunatic Asylum—Aldermen Hornbrook, Jarvis, Littleton, Love, Risdon, and Waycott. Councillors Birch, Charlick, Heard, Jane, W. J. May, Olver, Phillips, Roberts, Viggers, and Welsford.

Parks—Aldermen Jolliffe, Risdon, and Waycott. Councillors Archer, Birch, Chappell, Cole, Essenhigh, George, Jackson, Jenkin, Moon, Olver, Roberts, Treglohan, and Welsford.

Sanitary—Aldermen Jarvis and Leest. Councillors Baxter, Daymond, Doney, Goodman, Heard, Hellen, Jane, Littleton, W. J. May, McDonald, Rudall, Screech, Viggers, and Weeks.

Surveyors—Alderman Cousins. Councillors Charlick, Cole, Daymond, George, Hocking, Jackson, Littleton, Moon, Olver, Perkins, Phillips, Roberts, Screech, Smith, and Watson.

Tramways—Aldermen Fredman, Jolliffe, Tozer, and Waycott. Councillors Archer, Birch, Cole, Doney, Essenhigh, Heard, Hocking, W. J. May, McDonald, Smith, Tozer, and Welsford.

Watch—Aldermen Cousins, Day, Fredman, Hornbrook, Jarvis, Jolliffe, and Risdon. Councillors Birch, Daymond, Hellen, Littleton, Moses, Perkins, Screech, Smith, and Weeks.

Water—The Mayor. Aldermen Fredman, Gill, Hornbrook, Jarvis, Jolliffe, Leest, and Littleton. Councillors Baxter, Clarke, Mayne, Moon, Phillips, Rudall, Watson, and Weakford.

As Safe As Houses?

Not quite. A runaway tram down Albert Road swayed very dangerously. The brave driver stuck to his post, stamping his foot on the bell all the way down. When the vehicle reached the bottom it left the rails and ran straight across into Sparrow Park hitting the shelter. Fortunately the locals had quickly bolted from it when they heard the commotion from the oncoming tram belting downhill towards them. The conductor of this tram, hanging on the side, is William Voss.

The Devonport County Borough Police, 1909-1910

Among those seated at the rear of Ker Street Guildhall is Mrs. Gribbell's grandfather, Inspector Joseph Voss. Note the military style hat that Chief Constable. J. H. Watson is wearing.

Carnival Time

Devonport people thoroughly enjoyed the carnival. Here, wearing a trilby and standing on the running board, is Mr. Len Baldwin who was a member of the Carnival Committee in the 1930s. This was one of the many floats that took part in the raising of money to help the Royal Albert Hospital that was supported by voluntary contributions.

Boomps a Daisy

Margaret Morris (now Tarr) sings a favourite song of the 1930s, *Hands, Knees and Boomps-a-Daisy*. Whether singing solo on stage, or singing and dancing in large numbers, the pupils of Geraldine Lamb's School of Dancing gave enormous pleasure to those fortunate enough to be enjoying on afternoon sitting in the enclosure in Devonport Park during carnival week.

The "Starlight" Concert Party.

ALL

REFRESHMENTS

supplied at the

PARK PAVILION

as, Minerals and Home-made Ices

Park Pavilion

What better way to finish a pleasant summer's afternoon, having listened to the *Starlight Concert Party*, than to stroll up past the bandstand and over to have some refreshments at the Park Pavilion.

THE YOUNG ARTISTES appearing in these Delightful Dancing Displays are appearing through the kindness of Miss Geraldine Lamb, of the Cobourg School of Dancing, Cobourg St., Plymouth.

These clever young children are all pupils of this very popular School and are always in great demand in the West. They have appeared at all the leading Theatres in the City, and have had the honour of appearing and playing in Sir Frank Benson's Company at the Theatre Royal on several occasions. Speciality Dancing Acts, Children's Leads, Troupes, Chorus Ensembles, Ballets, etc., have been supplied to all the prominent local Theatres, and have always been a great attraction in Pantomime.

They have earned a reputation second to none in the City for their readiness to provide a show or entertainment for any deserving cause or charity, when they give their services and time entirely free.

During the past few years they have given over 1,000 such performances in the City and other parts of the West.

Another notable enterprise of this up-to-date School has been the Production for Five years running of their own Pantomimes culminating in a great presentation of RED RIDING HOOD at the popular Alhambra Theatre.

Day Number One

Mr. E. Ellery, fourth from the left, worked in the Dockyard as a blacksmith. On his way to work he joined the spectators as the first war memorial in Devonport Park was erected. The fearsome looking pom-pom gun was captured from the Boers in the Battle of Paardeberg in 1900. It commemorates men who died in a military engagement but were all Naval personnel of H.M.S. *Doris*. Note the planks lying beside the three-recessed marble panels. The high wall at the rear of the gun is no longer part of the horizon.

Cruising Up the River, 1932

The Herbert Street Methodist Boating Club on a trip up the river Tamar to Weir Head. Those enjoying the voyage were Bob Lewis, Rev. Morelle, Bill Weymouth, Fred Williams, Edgar Bird, Beatrice Moore and Kath Down. The boat *Herbert* was a pre-1930 clinker-built naval boat fitted with an engine. This is part of the club sitting "aft". Herbert Street Church was blitzed in 1941.

Buy Your Badges Here, 3d each

The author is standing with Bill Massey, Alf Rothery and Fred Merrin, outside the selling centre, which was temporarily erected outside Sparrow Park across from the bottom of Albert Road. There were special weeks to aid the war effort: (1941) War Weapons, (1942) Warships Week, (1943) Wings for Victory, (1944) Salute the Soldier, and (1945) Thanksgiving Week. Impressive parades by the Services and Civil Defence organisations also took place.

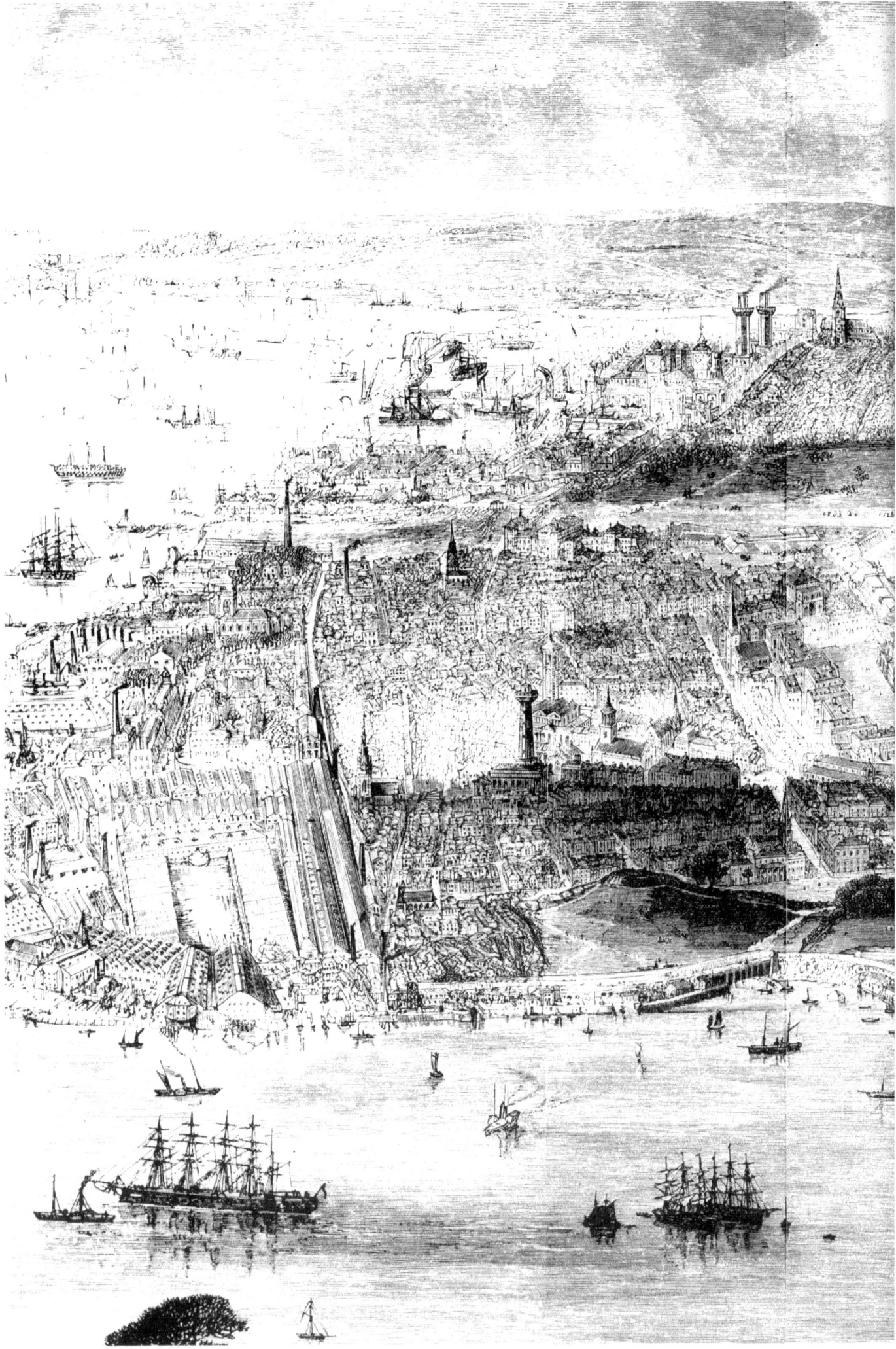

Map showing Lines of Fortifications in 1871.

Call the Fire Brigade!

Gilbert, the "Call out Boy" could be seen rushing up Ker Street Ope. On reaching Ker Street at the side of the Guildhall the housing for the fire-engine would be facing him. In the photo it is seen on the left of the Guildhall (facing). After looking at the blackboard in Ker Street fire-station he would see where the fire was and then run shouting, "Fire at Fore Street!" The Devonport Voluntary Fire Brigade, as it was known until amalgamation in 1914, had horses to pull the engine. Mr. James Symons, a gas inspector, was in the fire brigade along with other civilians such as Tommy Evans, and the Crocker brothers.

A Handsome Residence

This for many years was the residence of the Port Admiral, known as the Commander-in-Chief. All public business connected with the service was conducted here with the exception at one time of courts martial which took place on board the Guard-ship. The beautiful steeple of St. Stephens Church is seen on the left. Mr. C. Fox and Mr. E. Drake remember the nearby Johnston Memorial Hall, that at one time was used for drama and by pensioners for their recreation.

Curtis V.C.

Philip Curtis, who was born in Devonport, won his Victoria Cross for continuing to charge the enemy though badly wounded. He continued attacking until dead. He was killed in Korea during the 1950s. Here he is seen at James Street. It was taken in the back of the flats, when he was about six years old. Terry Clifford is on the left and then Philip Curtis. Bill Clifford is behind. Lily Oaks is holding one of the shields. St. John's Street was renamed Curtis Street in honour of Devonport's V.C.

Turkeys at 1/8d

David Greig had three shops, one in Union Street, Cornwall, Street, Plymouth, and another in Fore Street, Devonport. All the shop fronts were of the same design; burnt sienna marble with white marble. In the photograph Mrs. Esther Wills (née Symons, the sister of the signwriter who painted HIPPO on the roof of the Hippodrome) is in white overalls on the right of the door facing. Mr. Atwill, the Cornwall Street manager, is on the right and Sandercock of Devonport is the errand boy with peak cap.

The Ropery, late 19th Century?

Mr. Cyril Symons' relative was Mrs. Emma Spry, who was charge women of the Ropery in 1924 in the Dockyard. Women were also employed in the sail loft. The Ropery was used by the Royal Dockyard Sunday School for Christmas parties. There had to be plenty of bunting as it is such a long building. Mrs. Spry would take a tommy basket with her to carry her lunch. She lived at Ker Street.

A Member of the A.T.S., 1942

Anne Voss, now Mrs. Thomas of Devonport, is standing outside the Devonport Library building in Duke Street. The Women of the Auxiliary Territorial Service gave magnificent help to the country's defence during the war. Many of them helped to crew the anti-aircraft guns.

Strolling in Fore Street

Mr. Pat Ghillyer, with cap at a jaunty angle, is enjoying a walk with a friend in Fore Street. The half-moon sign of the Tivoli can be seen on the opposite side of the road. Pat in 1936 became the chief operator of the Tivoli, which opened in 1909 when Mr. L. Frost took over the former auction rooms in Fore Street and converted them into a silent picture house.

Cornwall Street, the Oldest Street in Devonport

A house in Cornwall Street, situated at the top on the left-hand side going down towards North Corner, received first prize for the best decorated house in the carnival of the early twenties.

THE DEVONPORT I REMEMBER
P. F. Ghillyer

Cornwall Street, The Oldest Street in Devonport

I was born in this famous street in 1914 for which I can claim the title of being a *Cornwall Street Arab*. This street in its heyday was a very close knitted street. Families from top to bottom all helped each other in times of distress or bereavement. The lower half of the street consisted mainly of boating families, descending from generations of sea-faring men. When as small kids, we used to give a hand with the various baskets of produce off loaded from many kinds of steamers which called at North Corner from Botus Fleming, Cargreen and many other places. The quay was a beehive of activity. Whitfields, the carriers, with their horse-drawn carts, were to be seen going up and down Cornwall Street all day on Saturdays taking the produce and goods to Devonport market.

On the sombre side of life, we kids witnessed more than once, the arrival down Cornwall Street of two very large policemen from the Ker Street station pushing what seemed to be a large basket fixed to the chassis of a four-wheeled pram. This long basket was made to hold a corpse. The policemen were on their way down to North Corner to collect the body of a drowned person. The body was kept at the rear of the old pier master's lovely red-brick victorian building which still stands. We would walk alongside the burly policeman when pushing the body back up Cornwall Street en route to the small annexe mortuary by the old Guildhall.

We also saw family feuds settled with bare fist fights between the two heads of families. These took place either down on the beach (when the tide was out) or else in the back lane. At most times the fighters stripped to the waist and, being cheered on by the respective members of the opposing families, were swelled by onlookers from the rest of the street. The mêlée usually ended with a couple of bleeding noses and bruised faces and a shake of hands on both sides.

I remember the famous fire in the well known stables of the Devonport Mineral Water Company in 1924 (in the middle of the night too). Brigades from Ker Street fire station and other stations arrived and the horses were saved by one modest chappie, George (Bogey) Dart, who is still alive and resides in the Stonehouse area. He should have received a medal many years ago!

Annual Carnival

We had our street decorated for the 1925 carnival and it truly looked magnificent. People came from all over the place just to tour round and see it. We had nice shops on both sides of the street and four public houses, the main one being at the top called the *Cambridge*. The other two are still here, the *Steam Packet Inn* and the *Swan*. The fourth went many years before the last war. The street also had four of those old fashioned lamp posts and we would watch the lamplighter come round every evening, lighting each with his long handled pole which held a flame at its top. At the declaration of World War II boys were asked to climb these lamp posts and turn off the gas light to help towards the blackout. Leslie Hore Belisha came to this very street in his car during the 1920s to give out toys to the very poor children. He was later elected as the liberal M.P. for Devonport. Another incident remembered by us all was the Plymouth Corporation horse-drawn dustcart down on North Corner quayside back in 1928. The brake slipped and the cart rolled backwards and pulled the horse and refuse with it into the Tamar which was at high tide. Men dived into the water and struggled to release the horse from its harness which they did just in time. The cart sank between North Corner pontoon and the quay wall. When the tide went out a hawser was hooked to the cart and it was hoisted up by a crane to the cobblestone quay, most of its contents spilling onto the mudflats. We watched the sea-soaked dustcard being pulled up through Cornwall Street by a corporation lorry on its way to Pottery Quay, the depot for the Devonport carts.

Shaky Bridge

The picture in part III of this series calls to mind the switchback bridge, otherwise known as *Shaky Bridge*, built of wood and crossing the estuary from where Camel's Head cinema stood. It crossed over to Westlake's monumental mason premises where there once stood a tin tram shed to hold a couple of open-roofed trams. As the bridge was too weak and shaky to carry a tram, Dockyardies who caught the tram from Saltash Ferry, had to alight at this point and cross over on foot then board another tram which was waiting opposite the old cinema. The bridge, of course, was eventually taken down and the present road constructed.

Alcester Street was a very classy street in its heyday and people used to come to admire the decorated mound of coloured porcelain and china stuck around a mound in one of the gardens. A photograph appeared in the *Herald* showing it sometime during the 1920s. A little old lady collected all kinds of china and cemented them onto this large mound in the front of her house. It really looked a thing of beauty but alas it has gone, although the house still stands.

Penlee Gardens were the homes of gentry when we were kids. They had their own tennis courts but the site has since been taken over by the fire brigade. The fine houses were owned by retired officers of the armed forces and lawyers and doctors. There used to be a very fierce gatekeeper on duty and he would not let anybody through unless they could prove their identity and purpose for visiting. He also had a dog.

I found Roy Watkin's article very interesting but I must correct him on one item. The *Pearl White* series of films were shown in the *Electric Theatre*, not the *Tivoli* which was under the management of Mr Boultwood from 1910 then Mr Frank Wheeler from 1920. However, the *Tiv* did have the first run of *Elmo Lincoln*, the first screened Tarzan and the *Eddie Polo* series were also a great attraction at the cinema as well.

Tram Accident

I also read with interest the notes on the old trams and recall in William Street, Morice Town, when one open-roof tram was swaying down towards Albert Road and suddenly its arm left the overhead wires and swung to the right crashing through three windows. The tram screeched to a halt but nobody was hurt. We had been looking at the stills outside the Morice Town picture house at the time. There was also another instance of a runaway tram, no. 25, which occurred on 27th November, 1914. It raced down through St Michael's Terrace full of Dockyardies coming off the night shift. It left the rails at the junction of Paradise Road and went straight across and hit the wall of the London and South West Railway. The patched-up wall can still be seen and some of the passengers were injured.

Dockyard Bell

The dockyard hooter was also mentioned. In my time the policeman on duty at the main gate in Fore Street rang a bell starting at 6.50 a.m. It stopped ringing dead on 7 a.m. and all "Yardies" had to be within the walls or else! The hooter was installed some years later. Many of the old Cornwall Street arabs congregated outside the gates at 5 p.m. to ask for any bread or buns left over. Most of the kids had no shoes on their feet and they came from very poor families. The much loved firm of Messrs. Prynns, of Tavistock Street, started to take provident cheques in order to help these poor families. Messrs. Prynns were later known as the "champion of the poor of Devonport".

Stephens/Risdons, Marlborough Street. Alderman Solomon Stephens, *Solly Stephens* to us all in Devonport, used to let the poor come up to his house and buy stale buns and cakes. He wore two pairs of spectacles! As he sat at his cash desk he "lorded" over everything going on. We kids sat on the rails of Stonehouse Bridge when the tolls were lifted in 1924. Tolls were also abolished at Millbridge. Alderman Stephens became Mayor twice.

During my time the *Cambridge Hotel* and public house was run by Mr and Mrs T. Madigan, the parents of my colleague Tom Madigan who was the last superintendent of the births, marriages and deaths office at the old Plymouth Registry. We grew up together in Cornwall Street but Tom was not allowed to come out and play with myself or other boys. The Band of Hope Chapel, now the Armada Club, was popular with the kids for its magic lantern shows taking many of them off the streets during the long autumn and winter evenings.

This once glorious street, known to sea-faring men from all over the world, was compulsory purchased in 1936 for future development and families who had lived there for years were moved to the nearly erected council houses at St Budeaux. Council flats were later built on the site of the many 200 year old three-storey houses which faced the street. Another reminder of the area is the old Infants' School halfway down on the right.

The Ram Procession

On Boxing Day during the 1920s and many years before my generation was born, there used to be a procession around the streets of Devonport. Its acquired the name, *The Ram*, but no one knows why or when it started. Apparently it had been taking place for many years. Two well known boating families of Morice Town, Swabey and Blight, supplied the act and music and the elders of the families dressed up in circus clown costumes with their faces painted. One held a large accordion and the others accompanied it in singing. Another of the team carried a Christmas tree, beautifully decorated, while others carried collecting boxes the proceeds of which went to the Old Royal Albert Hospital, Devonport. Everyone of my age can remember the Boxing Day procession of *The Ram* through all the streets of Devonport. Many high churchmen took a dim view of the verses saying the whole thing was a parody of the Way of the Cross of our Lord in Jerusalem. This was always denied by the organisers. A few lines are quoted in this book on another page.

Annual Bonfire

Always on 5th November night the boys would collect loads of firewood for the huge bonfire which was always sited on the beach. Times would be planned when the tide was out. In some years it was early in the evening, in others the fire would not be lit until 9.30 p.m. Crowds used to come from all over the place because these annual Cornwall Street bonfires were huge affairs topped up very high with many weeks spent beforehand by the arabs in obtaining materials for the blaze. It was kept in stores in Holman's buildings at the rear of the street. The event itself always turned into a real street party. There were never any accidents, no drunks and no drugs! No muggings took place or handbags stolen. Those were the best days of the golden age of old Devonport!

Daddy Netting

Four doors down from the *Cambridge* was an antique shop owned and run by an elderly gentleman called Netting. We kids gave him the nickname *Wire netting*. His shop was stuffed with countless curios, ornaments, nick-nacks and guns of various descriptions. Burglars broke in on one occasion but did not find old Daddy Netting's money. They took binoculars and other goods. The police asked him why the burglars did not find his money (he never believed in banks). It was well known that he kept money in his house. It appeared that he changed his weekly takings into Bradbury pound notes and also the white £5 notes which he carefully folded and stuck beneath the wooden slats of his venetian blinds. By keeping the blinds permanently up the money was well out of sight. The police, however, ordered him to lower the blinds and removed hundreds of pounds. He was later accompanied to the bank over in Fore Street and for the first time in his long life he was obliged to open an account. Netting looked like a character from one of Dicken's books. He wore a velvet skull cap with a gilt silk teasal attached and a long frock coat.

St. John's Girls School, 1915

Mr. Bone, who was a lawyer of Ker Street, took scripture lessons. First left in the front is Beatie Lake, who was the sister of Bugler Lake, Devonport's well-known champion boxer. Bugler Lake lived in Monument Street. He went to the Johnny Williams' Boxing Club in Cherry Garden Lane which was at the rear of one of Fore Street's shops. Len Harvey also went there.

Morice Town School, 1916–17

Some of the boys shown here have been recognised. They are William Feabes, Leslie Harris and Charles Prideaux. Note also the two boys in sailor clothes. The Girls' Junior School was opposite the Wesleyan Church on the corner of Albert Road and Charlotte Street. The Boys' Junior School was behind the girls' and was reached by going down a flight of steps between the Infant and Junior Schools.

The Matchbox House

The time is spring and the year 1934 and the place is Somerset Place School. The red matchbox house was made by Miss Bosworthick one of the teachers. On the left of the house: Raymond Haley, Ron, Peter Hill, Joan, Desmond Damerell. On the right: Betty Porter, John Brock, Hazel, Pamela Baker, Alex Payne and Christine Weeks. Children also attended from the Scattered Homes which at one time was situated where the flats are at the top of Ford Hill. Girls from the orphanage in Albert Road marched two by two to attend the school.

There's Something About A Soldier

Hundreds of people in Devonport would be waiting to see the troops. Marching behind their bands they would leave the parade ground and follow the baton-twirling drum major into Cumberland Road. The Raglan Barracks had squares named George, Cumberland, Ligonier and Frederick. Mr. Pat Ghillyer remembers visiting the stables when a boy and looking at the mules that used to draw the four-wheeled gun carriages. They were a popular sight both in Raglan and Granby (on the opposite side of Fore Street) Barracks.

Come Listen to the Band

The 1st Devonshire Regiment is playing to the delight of numerous adults and children that used to visit the Lines each Sunday morning for such a treat. Young children would go around to the cookhouse where they would be given a flat tin of tough army oatmeal biscuits. There were five biscuits to a tin, and they nearly broke one's teeth when an attempt was made to chew through them.

Fall In!

In the Brickfields background the London and S.W. Railway (now the College of Further Education) can be seen. In 1920 five soldiers climbed over the high wall of Raglan Barracks on the Chapel Street side. They intended to desert. They all dropped down the other side, but one broke a leg and all five were rounded up once the alarm was sounded. They were given a court-martial. Apart from the soldiers in Raglan Barracks the nearby Granby Barracks housed soldiers of the artillery and cavalry.

The First House

Until 1700 the town had not been commenced, not a house was to be seen except the barton-house of Mount Wise which stood on the summit, once occupied by the semaphore. The first house of the town was at North Corner. There is a ball hoisted at the signal station. Could this have been the signal to fire the old gun at one o'clock each day? This photograph shows the Admiral's Steps which were built in 1820 before the construction of the pier.

MOUNT WISE, DEVONPORT.

MOUNT WISE BATHING HOUSES, DEVONPORT

Pikeys

To get to Pikeys, the nickname given to the old swimming baths, men and boys would walk across the Mount Wise parade, and at the end of the expanse of gravel would view one of the most beautiful of scenes before walking down the slope towards the five-sided wooden signal. This beacon of coloured glass was the Admiralty's signal for ships coming through the Western King's narrows.

A Walk by the Sea

Mrs. L. Hooper has just walked down the narrow path (still in existence) from Richmond Walk. At one time small cottages were sited here. Boys, having finished a game of five stones at Pikeys and having called at Clara Flemings at the small shop near Blagdons Boats to buy some sweets, would make their way to the small beach (to the left of the photo where the small steps still exist) to meet mothers for a picnic. The nearby swings, including a maypole with metal chains and metal hand-grips, would complete the day.

Mutton Cove

The watermen at Mutton Cove used to load their boats and take passengers over to Mount Edgcumbe. When they arrived they would go through a pay-stile in a triangular part of the beach and walk up to the obelisk field for a picnic. The watermen also took sailors back to their ships. On the right of the photograph is the spot where the author, at the age of four, was saved from drowning by the quick action of one of the watermen.

The Golden Hind, June, 1938

The original 120 ton *Golden Hind* was reputed to have had 18 guns, some firing a two-pound shot 500 yards. The half-scale model of Sir Francis Drake's famous ship is at anchor at Mutton Cove's pier. The door of Sibley's Wagonettes is on the right of the steps (facing). Thousands of people watched the *Golden Hind* at H.M.S. *Drake* during Navy Week. Drake was the first Englishman to circumnavigate the globe. The first man to circumnavigate the world in both directions was Captain Tobias Furneaux who was born at Swilly, now North Prospect.

Sibley's Waggonettes

Sibley's Waggonettes from Mutton Cove were as much a part of old Devonport as the statue of King Billy. They supplied all the old fashioned transport, the lovely horses always having shiny coats. Most people seemed to know about the magnificent Sibley coaches that attended such functions as Tavistock Goose Fair. Mr. Sibley is seen here with two of his horses. Reg and Arthur Baser remember Sibley's Wagonettes joining in the processing around Devonport during the celebrations when Bugler Lake won the championship. Andrew Stephen, manager of Alfords Grocery shop in Marlborough Street blew the post horn sitting in front.

The Queen of Rumania visits Devonport in 1925.

It was all Happening in the Twenties
Queen of Rumania visits Devonport, 1925

The Queen was visiting the Alexandra Maternity Home at Stoke, opposite Devonport Park. Among the crowd was Mr. Bundy of the C.I.D. (to the right of flag) and Sammy Lucan of St. Aubyn Street, also a member of the C.I.D. Marjorie Laxton remembered seeing "the really regal lady in an expensive blue gown, with beautiful dark hair", visiting the Commander in Chief at Mount Wise. Mr. Pat Ghillyer writes "She was the daughter of the Duke of Edinburgh when he was Commander in Chief at Mount Wise. Marie used to play with her little friends on the well known bronze cannon which used to be on the top of Mount Wise slope (opposite the Captain Scott Memorial), pointing out to sea. Sentries were instructed to keep a very watchful eye on Marie, the daughter whose father laid the foundation stone of the old Smeaton Tower when re-erected on the Hoe and the foundation stone of the new wing of the Naval Orphanage at the top of Albert Road, the building later to be occupied by the D. of E. Directorate. In years to come, Marie married the King of Rumania, and was known to Devonport people as "Marie of Rumania". My sister and I sat on the rails at King's Road in 1925 when Queen Marie drove up in her car en-route to visit the maternity homes at St. Michael's Terrace, Stoke. On that day there were crowds of people all waiting to see her. The car procession must have consisted of about ten vehicles. Marie waved to us all. In those carefree young days she was popular with the people of this country as well as abroad."

With Alan Cobham 1924

First Boy to Fly over Plymouth, ran the headline of a local newspaper. Young Arthur Baser, whose home was at Corporation Buildings, Morice Square, had the honour of being the first Plymouth boy to fly over his native town. Arthur, who ran errands for Solomon Stephens of Marlborough Street, flew on the "Ten shillings a flight" with the world famous pilot at Roborough.

Electric Theatre

The sign *Electric Theatre* is displayed just above the tram. It stood opposite the Tivoli cinema which also had its own smart commissionaire. Before 1910 The Theatre building was the Public Hall. After 1910 it became a cinema. It had a large stone wall screen on the Devonport Park side wall. Therefore, those in the gallery on the Fore Street side had to have their eyes turned right to watch the screen. In 1932 it became a new cinema and was built further along Fore Street incorporating the YMCA. *Trader Horn* was one of the first films shown. Look past the women in flowing dress. A bit of the "Main Guard", as the elderly locals still call it in Fore Street, can be seen before improvements in the early 1920s took place.

The Hospital, Royal Naval Barracks, Devonport.

The Admiralty Regret to Announce...

"... the loss of H.M.S. *Gipsy*." In 1939, during the beginning of the war, the names of the ships lost were broadcast by the B.B.C. On hearing the news, anxious wives would hurry into the Royal Naval Barracks, while the children waited at home. Fortunate relatives would find the survivors in the hospital of the barracks. There was no "phoney" war period for the naval men of Devonport who were in the thick of battle from the war's beginning. High explosive bombs fell on Boscawen Block during the war killing many sailors.

Keep in Step!

Youngsters from Devonport had the time of their lives during Navy Weeks before the war of 1939. Having paid their entrance fee inside the main gate of the Royal Naval Barracks, they were soon watching the "Battle of Jutland", being re-enacted by model ships coupled with realistic bangs. Later, in one of the Dockyard basins, a submarine would surface. After being "hit" by shells fired by one of the surface ships, the submarine would "sink", after some of the crew had dived overboard.

R.N. BARRACKS, KEYHAM.

BLUEJACKET BAND, ROYAL NAVAL BARRACKS, DEVONPORT

Bluejackets Band

The free and easy attitude of the sailor ashore would belie the smartness of the sailors in the band or those marching behind it. The Royal Navy has always encouraged those with an interest in music. The Royal Naval Artificer Apprentices Band of H.M.S. *Fisgard* was often seen in the streets of Devonport wearing smart white gloves and marching with precision.

Arthur L. Clamp – the man behind the books

Arthur Leslie Clamp was a man of boundless energy with a passion for helping others, particularly through his love of history. A printer by trade, he started his career in a printing company before moving his family from Exeter to Plymouth to teach at the Plymouth College of Art and Design, where he eventually became the Head of the Printing Department.

Arthur with his five children.

A Devoted Family Man

Despite his love of teaching, Arthur prioritised his family, always making it home by 5:30pm for tea. He and his wife, Rosemary, raised five children: Susan, Angela, Elizabeth, David, and Steven. Arthur would often combine his love of family and history by taking his children on Sunday walks, encouraging them to appreciate historical monuments by taking photos or making crayon rubbings of gravestones for his books. The family home at 203 Elburton Road was a hub of activity, with a large garden, featuring a two-storey fort and a makeshift swimming pool.

A Lifelong Learner and Adventurer

Arthur's thirst for knowledge extended beyond history to a deep curiosity about the world. He was passionate about exploring different cultures, traditions, and cuisines, often taking advantage of his long summer holidays as a teacher to travel to places like India, Russia, South America, the middle east and the USA, sometimes bringing one of his children along. This adventurous spirit even influenced his home life, as seen by the short-lived family tradition of steam-cooking vegetables after a trip to Iceland.

History is a prominent feature of family days out

Community and Philanthropic Spirit

His commitment to serving others was evident in his long-standing involvement with the Elburton Methodist Church. He was the Sunday School Superintendent for over 15 years and served as the editor of the wider church's monthly newsletter, "The Link," for a similar duration. After Rosemary's very sad passing, Arthur later remarried and, following a chance encounter with a professor from India, established a connection with a missionary school in Chennai. Together with his new wife, Christine, he co-founded a "Sponsor a Child's Education" program that continues to this day.

Pictured left – The cover of 'The Link' complete with hand drawn sketches of each church by Angela
Below right – Arthur Clamp promoting his latest book
Below left – Arthur at home with his first wife, Rosemary
Below centre – Arthur on holiday with his second wife, Christine

A Legacy of Learning and Positivity

Arthur's greatest passion was history, which he brought to life through tireless research, documentation, and the many books he authored. He was driven by a need to "never be stuck in a rut," constantly seeking new experiences, meeting new people, and expanding his knowledge. With a positive attitude and a great sense of humour, he was always ready to help others, leaving a lasting impact on his family and community. His children, Susan, Angela, Elizabeth, David, and Steven, remember him with love and gratitude.

David Clamp, 2025

A Legacy of Local History

Below is the story of how Arthur L Clamp began writing books, in his own words, drafted shortly before he passed away in 2001. I have only made minor alterations to this text, correcting grammatical errors that he did not survive to correct himself. When I first discovered this text, I was shocked to see my name mentioned. It seems that, unbeknownst to me, I shared my first PC with him. I suspect he used it during the day when I was at school, although I do have one memory of sitting with him and showing him how it worked. It has been a pleasure to pick up where he left off and see his books republished and redistributed, and to know that I was part of the story, even back then. It was also fascinating to discover that his pricing structure matches the way I have tried to price the books, with a third going to local sellers and the rest covering printing costs with a little left over for my expenses.

I am his eldest grandson, and it is a privilege to curate his legacy, which we are calling 'The Clamp Collection'. The very last line of the text originally reads "The following pages list all the titles." Sadly, that page is missing and we have no record of all the books he published and knowing that some of those were researched by other authors makes the process of finding them even harder. I look forward to one day completing the collection and seeing them all available again. And maybe, one day, I'll even start writing my own to add to the series. For now, here is his story in his own words.

Steven Gibson, 2025

Writing and Publishing Booklets on Local Topics and Areas

I started this interest in either 1968 or 1969 when living in Woodford. I had by these dates established the Department of Printing and I think I must have been looking for something different to do. The first titles were of A5 size proofed from type set at Clarke, Doble and Brendon, Ltd., Plymouth printers, and then made up into pages and printed at Sawtell and Neilson, Ltd., Totnes.

Then began a slow process of getting them out to shops, etc. which proved to be more time consuming and difficult than actually researching, writing and getting the books into print. However, I persisted and opened a business account with Barclays Bank on the Broadway. I was advised to give it a title so I called it "Westway Publications". There came along another problem, one of storage of paper and finished books which was solved when the family moved to Elburton in 1970.

I changed the printer to Penwell, Ltd., Callington, Cornwall, as he was then just setting up himself and his prices seemed very reasonable. I did not get any of the printers to make up the complete books. I hand folded the flat printed sheets, stitched the books on a small manual table stitcher and trimmed them in a small hand turned guillotine which I bought from someone in Penzance for £40. It was brought up in a van.

The trouble and time going to and fro to Callington was too much so I transferred the printing to PDS Printers, Prince Rock, Plymouth, and I have been with them ever since. Now they are at Plympton which is easy to reach and they fold the flat sheets which was turning out to be a long chore which only saved a small part of the printing costs.

All my first titles were written by myself. I took the photographs and developed them in the loft of the house, the type was set by now on a computer situated in the house at Elburton from which I had collected photographic lengths of text to cut up and law down as pages.

At some point I decided that I would do my own film processing of lith film so I bought a large second hand process camera from Kingsbridge and learnt through trial and error to make line negatives of the text and halftone negatives of the illustrations which proved more difficult than I anticipated. The main problem was trying to keep the developer in the large dish at the correct temperature as any change would affect the developing time. I replaced this old camera with a brand new one bought from Croydon, Surrey, costing £900. This has turned out to be a great asset cutting out an expensive part of the printer's costs and one crucial aspect of the work which I could control.

By the middle 1970s there were many outlets I had contacted in Plymouth, up to Dartmoor, Exeter, around to Torbay, Totnes, Dartmouth and the South Hams. The market for local books was much greater than I had first thought and through getting to know many local people undertaking research themselves had the chance to help and make up books for other people who had in most instances, got together a collection of photographs with some text in a rather muddled way. Through my experience in print I was able to shape up their work and get it into print and in every case I had to pay the printer and let the person have the royalties. In the majority of titles produced in this manner this was another way of producing titles and it did give some profit to my work. However, I must say that in a few cases I lost out by either the other person getting the numbers wrong, not returning any monies from stock I delivered or they thought that more of their books should have been sold.

The print run was usually 1,000 copies and from time to time I have had reprints of 250 copies. It took about ten years to clear the first print run so I always had large stocks in the garage, workshop, etc. The numbers sold during the early years was about 7,000 copies a year increasing to around 9,000 copies and for the whole of the enterprise about 500,000 have been sold. The booklets have become part of the local scene and many people collect them, shops regularly order copies and I go around certain areas month by month restocking or replacing titles as necessary.

During the past year or so I have started setting the text on a Packard Bell PC, something which I should have done some years back. I share it with Steven Gibson, my grandson. There appears to be no end to the market for local books, but I could not earn a regular income because of the long time it takes to sell stock.

However, now exceeding 100 titles made up mainly of A4 twenty-four page booklets, some folded guides, with selling prices set with a third going to the shop which is the trade custom, the original idea has been quite successful and could go on for ever.

Apart from monetary benefits, however spasmodically these might be, I have learnt a lot myself, met many interesting people and have become part of the local scene with requests to give talks and to advise people about getting into print.

Arthur L Clamp, 2001

Death of local historical author

'He was an incredible character who was just loved by everybody who knew him'

This newspaper article, published by the Evening Herald on 17th August 2001, forms a good record of his life. Just as he encourages us to learn more about local history, we encourage you to learn a little about him. For that reason, we have included these pages at the back of all the most recently republished books, in honour of his memory and recognition of his contribution to the community.

www.ingramcontent.com/pod-product-compliance
Lightning Source LLC
Chambersburg PA
CBHW061407070526
44584CB00031B/4179